some perverse verse

John Treneman

Published by John Treneman
55 Foley Road
Claygate
Surrey KT10 0LU

First published 2007

Copyright © John Treneman 2007

The right of the author has been asserted

All rights reserved.
No part of this publication may be reproduced, stored in or
inroduced into a retrieval system, or transmitted, in any form
or by any means (electronic, mechanical, photcopying,
recording or otherwise), without the written permission
of the author.

ISBN 978-0-9541386-1-5

Set in Baskerville with Hoefler Text Ornament

Printed and bound by CPI Anthony Rowe

some
perverse
verse

CONTENTS

Themes	Poem numbers
Growing up	1 to 9
Life & death	10 to 20
O tempora	21 to 35
Beasts & Dreams	36 to 43
Whimsy	44 to 53
Romance	54 to 64

Growing up

ॐ

Contents

1. This little girl
2. Life's journey
3. Christmas Eve
4. Summer 1938
5. Prep school
6. Thankyou, Sir
7. An ordinary boy
8. Resolutions
9. A troubador I'd like to be

1. This little girl

This little girl had four brothers
And an old teddy bear on her knee
She grew up and married my father
Bore two little girls, and had me

Her father was fond of his daughter
Early mornings they'd go for a walk
I'm so sorry that I never knew him
As he died just before I could talk

Her mother looks grim in the portrait
Could it be that her belt was too tight?
Did she guess the Great War was coming
And her boys would go off to the fight?

The four boys returned safe and sound
To start up new lives back in Blighty
Their sister by now was a flapper
Did they think she'd become rather flighty?

This little girl played the piano
Lullabies for her children in bed
When family fortunes were troubled
She learned typing to bring in some bread

She brought us up minding our manners
And always to say what is true
Much more she explained by example
To be thoughtful in all that you do

She worked until she was eighty
Seemed surprised when they asked her to go
Missed the office as well as the income
But made sure that her mind didn't slow

It's some time since she went to her Maker
Away from the world and its strife
But her children still think of their mother
Who taught them so much about life

2. Life's journey

Baby's growing every day
He talks already --in his way

That boy has hollow legs Mum thinks
To judge by all the food he sinks

His teenage voice has gone quite deep
It's noon and yet he's still asleep

I wonder what he does at College
Maybe, with beer, he soaks up knowledge?

He's found a job, gets paid quite well
It seems his know-how rings the bell

A mortgage and a lovely flat
A lovely girl, too, sharing that

For years and years the couple tarried
But finally they upped and married

And now the two have found the way
Their baby's growing every day

3. Christmas Eve
ເຂ

Is Father Christmas coming here tonight?
Ask little children eager for their toys.
He will, my dears, when I put out the light
If you lie still and don't make any noise!
Downstairs the grownups pile parcels in a heap,
Fill stockings with those silly little things,
Knock back a dram or two to help them sleep,
Deaf to the song the hissing Yule log sings.
Outside the moon is shining on the snow
The sparkling stars are dancing round and round
The reindeer snort, bells jingling as they go
And Santa laughs--hush, can't you hear the sound?
     May peace and love now swaddle all the earth
     As Mary cared for Jesus at His birth

4. Summer 1938, Torbay
ເຂ

The spiders on their morning webs
Hang diamonds out to dry
Their glitter icily warns flies
And midges to pass by

The deep red bells of fuschia ring
And sway in summer's breeze
Their tongues hang downwards yellow-tipped
To attract the bumble bees

Grey concrete steps lead up to the house
The galvanised rail at the side
Feels smooth and cool on your cheek
But it's cooler still inside

The sitting-room is where you wait
Upon a plump settee
It's soft as soft, and yet it pricks
Horsehair behind the knee

Along one wall the piano stands
Pale Hands may strike a chord
'Beside the Shalimar' or 'Come
Into the garden, Maud'

The picnic's ready, and we walk
Down to the sea in the sun
At last we're there, we're on the beach
And the day has really begun!

5. Prep school
❧

There is to be no talking or playing in the bedrooms after the light has been taken away at night, or in the morning before the bell rings.

Night is a lonely time, and bed is a lonely place.

Dodds' round eyes were wet with tears
Everyone saw, but he's only six.
First night at school and the pillow is damp
Eyelids squeeze to stop the tears
Face down in the pillow to stifle the sobs
I'm nine and musn't let the others know !

Matthew Mark Luke and John
Guard the bed that I lie on
What shall I do if I need to wee?
The lights are out, but Matron's door
Is framed in light, and she looks cross

At Archer's sister's school, he says,
The girls are punished on bread and water.
We had boiled eggs for tea and Lucas's was raw
He thought he found a baby chick inside
And nobody wanted to finish their egg.

My feet are cold and I rub them together
But they slide like ice and don't get warm.
Night is a lonely time.

Matron's light is out.

Will morning ever come?

6. Thank you, Sir

You taught us mathematics
in a crazy kind of way
with puzzles that we fancied
making numbers seem like play

You looked a little crazy too
if you don't mind my saying so
you always answered questions
of the kind that made you go

away from the curriculum
to points of general knowledge.
Oh Sir, what is a bucket shop?
and when's a school a college?

In Trig the tipsy wasp
climbed four times round the glass:
we had to get the angle
-- Was it cider, Sir, or Bass?

I would have thanked you properly
if I'd known that you were going.
I still can't count for toffee, but
-- you taught me things worth knowing

7. An ordinary boy

This is the story of an ordinary boy
who really wants to meet a loving girl
he dreams of how he'll nuzzle in her hair
and run his fingers over smoothest skin

her hands, her arms, her ears,her neck, her cheek
and when it's time to part he'll kiss her mouth.

But when they meet no words are in his mouth
the man to be is still a callow boy
he wants to shine but hasn't got the cheek
to say hallo although he likes the girl,
admires the smoothness of her glowing skin
and gulps to see the sparkles in her hair.

He doesn't know it's sebum in her hair
that fillings jostle on the molars in her mouth.
He's worried 'cos of acne on his skin
he's nearly man but still too much a boy
but yet he knows she's just his sort of girl
she's got a wicked dimple in her cheek.

He shaved the new-grown bristles from his cheek
and started putting dressing on his hair.
His mother guessed he'd got himself a girl
and when she heard him gargling his mouth
she smiled: He's growing up, my little boy,
just like his Dad--same head, same neck, same skin.

That day, no dreaded acne blotched his skin
no stubble sprouted on his manly cheek
he knew his time had come, the happy boy!
Just down the street he recognised her hair
the words he needed came into his mouth
Hi, Lindy, will you be my special girl?

"Don't kiss my cheek, I want to taste your mouth
stop nuzzling my hair you greedy boy
I am your girl, be good to me, be good to me."

8. Resolutions

My mind's made up I'll have a go
at almost anything, you know
~~that's the joy of a new year

Smiling is fun, laughing is better
I mean to answer every letter
~~by return of post, my dear

I think I'll sail around the world
climb Everest with flag unfurled
~~and cut my toenails every week

I'll paint a picture for the Tate
I'll write a book that's really great
~~speak out my mind, stop being meek

I'll swim the Channel there and back
I'll bungee jump -- what the heck
~~there is no end of things to try

I'll cook the finest meal in town
I'll act in Shakespeare, play the clown
~~and every day more pigs will fly

I haven't mentioned being good
robbing the rich like Robin Hood
~~to give to the deserving poor

or founding hospitals and schools
and being tolerant to fools
~~on second thoughts don't ask for more

I'll have some training for my voice
and sing in opera for choice
~~to justify my taste for beer

Whatever next, I hear you say,
I can only beg and pray
~~that you won't check on me next year !

9. A troubador I'd like to be

A roundel

A Troubador I'd like to be
whose love-songs open every door
For food and drink (and maybe more)

He comes and goes a spirit free
obedient to no boring law
A troubador I'd like to be

His life is rich and full of glee
Unless his lordship with a roar
Takes offence and breaks his jaw
A Troubador ~~ who'd like to be?

Life & death

❧

Contents

10. A nun's tale
11. Flanders July 2005
12. Onions
13. Blessing
14. Mummy wasn't ill the day it snowed
15. The clouds are grand
16. Thanks
17. Duck thieves
18. Landfall
19. Holiday video
20. No choice at Dunblane

10. A nun's tale
෴

When I became a bride of Christ, my tears
were tears of joy, that safely here on earth
God would protect me, take away my fears
of marriage bed and pangs of childbirth.
Now, as the Abbess saw my flesh was weak
she took me from the pigsty cleaning chores
and set me in the sewing room to work
for God on lovely tapestries, indoors.
When good king William won his English fight
the Abbess gave us something new to sew.
With silken thread we told his story right
his men, his ships, his conquering the foe.
 My sin is pride, God knows, I cannot lie
 my needle 'twas that pierced King Harold's eye

11. Flanders -- July 2005
෴

Over the top on time they went
from muddy rat-infested trench
 to hell

They did their duty faithfully
(the generals did their very best
 as well)

And now, this summer's glorious day,
we cannot understand the how
 or why

As gravestones, line by domino line,
stand on parade, point hopefully at
 the sky

12. Onions

The ev'ning paper came just after three
She read it in the kitchen over tea
Page six announced Group Captain Smith was dead
Tears blurred her eyes as she remembered Fred

They'd met by chance the day he'd got his wings
They laughed and kissed and loved and talked of things
All summer, till the dreaded message came
MISSING+PRESUMED+KILLED...life could never be the same

The long months passed, it was no use to wait:
She'd married George -- he'd soon be at the gate
Her cheeks were wet, eyes red, what could she do?
Sharp knife, firm hand...peel onions for two

13. A Blessing for St Cecilia's Day

May the music of nature lighten all your ways
May a chorus of birds wake you up to the dawn
May you trill through your days like a lark on the wing
May good things come twice, like the wise thrush's song
May the nightingale's lullaby charm you to rest
Till you dance with the stars to the tunes of the blessed

14. Mummy wasn't ill the day it snowed

Mummy wasn't ill the day it snowed
The day I asked for help
The day we made the snowman

She rolled the snow into a great big ball
To start the body, then lumped more on
To lengthen it and shape the arms --
My little ball became the head.
Two coal-black eyes I gave him
And Mummy found a carrot for his nose.
And all the while the wind blew cold.

*   *   *

The cold wind blew on Mumy's lungs.

Or so the doctor said.

And the nurse.

And the Vicar at the funeral tea.

After that, the man we'd made began to cry.
I couldn't see or hear his tears
But he cried so much he shrank away
'Till only the coal unseeing eyes
And long limp carrot-nose were left,
Lifeless upon the ground.

*   *   *

Each time it snows upon her grave, I go to plant
Two coal-black eyes and a carrot-nose for her

But it makes no difference

15. The clouds are grand
❧

Back to the driver in a tip-up seat,
I do not look the others in the eye
For fear I might find myself unmanned
My sorrow showing uncontrollably.
I should have done my grieving earlier
In private, where I needn't feel ashamed.

So, as the car moves slowly down the street,
I look away and gaze up at the sky
And watch the changing clouds. They're a platoon
Of dragons breathing flames against a queen,
Then they are galleons anchored in a bay,
Now they're angels dancing a saraband.

'I love the clouds', she used to say to me.
'Their beauty's always changing, such a joy.
'Maybe you'll think of that when I am gone,
'My ashes scattered in some country field.'
As I remember this, I feel no need to cry.
What Mother said is true, the clouds are grand.

16. Thanks
❧

Thank 'ee kindly, the old man said.
The day they found him stuck in bed.
They packed his medicines with speed;
Thank you, he said, That's all I'll need.

In hospital they told him he should rest
But soon a doctor came, administered some test,
Pronounced him well, but needing care,
Warmth, food, a dressing-gown and chair.

Although he didn't really like the food,
Thank 'ee, he said, That meal was very good.
The day passed slowly, slower still the night:
Friends visited and found him not so bright.

His hearing failed, his sight was poor,
He dropped his bottle on the floor.
Nurse mopped it up, began to scold,
Thank you, he said, I'm getting old.

Then just as he was settled in
The bed was needed, not for him,
But for some patient far more ill:
A nursing home would keep him till...

Till when? Till he was fit for home
Once more to live (or die) alone?
Thank 'ee, he said with failing breath,
Shuddered, and gave his thanks to Death.

17. Duck Thieves
❦

Square head, white hair, pink face, straight eyes
Look out from the telly at me
And he tells how he and Charlie his friend
Went and stole a duck for their tea

The guards found out what Charlie'd done
And gave him a terrible beating
This was too much (but not enough!)
For the theft of a duck for eating

But not enough! "You friend, you come"
And fearful the friend was taken
To see poor Charlie on the ground
Bleeding and broken and shaking

"This man a thief, dishon'lable
Not worthy to die by sword
We get the cook with kitchen-knife
To do it, you mark my word."

The cook came out, a frightened man
He didn't quite understand
His body shook with mortal fear
And his knife shook in his hand

Not once, but twenty-seven times
Came down that kitchen-knife
And hacked and sliced at Charlie's neck
Until he escaped this life

"You friend, you take this now" they said
And with that they gave him the head
And Charlie's friend took up his spade
For the living must bury the dead

Square head, white hair, pink face, dry eyes
Looked out from the telly at me
As he told how he and Charlie his friend
Went and stole a duck for their tea.

(With acknowledgements to Arthur Titherington who narrated this incident on
the Channel 4 programme "Scars of War" on 20 August 1995)

18. Landfall

I've always enjoyed the view from the top
They say it's the journey that counts
More than arriving -- for me it is true
That the effort of climbing up high
Increases the pleasure I feel when I'm there.

There's the view, I can rest, and the air is like wine
Things below seem smaller yet clearer to me
In this moment of peace I'll examine my life
While I'm nearer than ever to heaven above

In the past, my laboured return from the top
Erased all too soon that moment of joy
But this time, yes this time I'll thrill
To adrenalin rush -- here I go-o-o-o

19. Holiday video

The brochures had promised a touch
Of romance in a time-locked world
Here olive-eyed womenb wear veils
While donkeys and mules carry loads
And the souk offers carpets and such
Our hotel provides plumbing (of sorts)
And international food
Whilst the company's man-on-the-spot
Says no problem is never too much

Here's the view from our room in the square
Can you see how the white roofs beyond
have turned pink in the evening sun,
Now it's morning -- you can't miss the sound
Of the muezzin's summons to prayer
That's me getting out of the bed
And bare-foot crossing the room
To open the shutters a crack
And savour the spice in the air

But notice the change down below.
That stage is set up in the square
And the people are crowding to see.
The official reads something aloud
Like a barker announcing a show,
I just managed to get into close-up
On this chap who is kneeling down there
Can you see the sweat on his face
As he waits for that terrible blow?

20. No choice at Dunblane

I canna' do what I want to do: they willna' let me

I have no friends at all in town
At least amongst the fully grown
They cross the street or look away,
Avoid me when I say Good-day

One year I ran a weekend camp
It rained, and when the lads got damp
Stuffy Authority found out
And wouldna' let me stay a Scoiut

Years later when I tried again
They wouldna' let me keep my men
Reports were on the file, they said
No matter what, my hopes were dead

I had to learn to play alone
A Lone Star Ranger with a gun,
Then suddenly it came to me
There was one way to make them see

I loaded up with all my gear
Surprised the enemy right here
And while she looked me in the eyes
I paid her back for all their lies

It seems the guns took over then
After the Captain, they went for the men
And when they'd finished, I drew breath..
There was no choice for me, but death

O tempora

Contents

21. Thought for today
22. Immigrants
23. Evolution
24. A farewell to the Olympics
25. Gladiators
26. Motorway blues
27. Thank you Columbus
28. David & Goliath
29. Chaucerian Roundel
30. Some thoughts on Identity
31. Poor Jack
32. A father's boast
33. A lament
34. Conversation piece
35. Home thoughts from abroad

21. Thought for today

In earliest times it seems to me
only one thing, the fruit of that tree,
was out of bounds, forbidden

Now life is changing all the time
it cries to be told in simple rhyme

The good book says thou shalt not steal
(but it may be okay to do a deal
that's rich for you and poor for them)

Thou shalt not kill so says the law
except if war's declared as just
(or government decides we must)

Pounds are out and kilos in
sex can be gay -- it is no sin
to broadcast it, once ten has struck

Lord, how they love to regulate
-- today what has by law to be straight
ain't sex -- it's carrots

Speaking of food big nanny says
eat less and less of what you like
sell the car and use a bike

Forget the fags cut down the booze
read all about it in the news
and come to that beware of fat

We're all of us told what we can't
but it's okay for us to want
to protest what others like to do

The strangest thing about a veto
is that it tempts the world and me to
do it anyway

22. Immigrants

Imprisoned when they reached these shores
They saw grey skies and felt the cold
    Poor strangers in a hostile land

Acclimatised, they then broke free
And formed their own community --
    Exotic ghetto from the South

Their gear's too bright for English eyes
And as for noise, they shriek enough
    To scare the blooming crows away

I'm not the only one who bleats
My next-door-neighbour grumbles too
    About these wretched parakeets!

23. Evolution
&

(June 2003)

Britain's getting crowded
not least in the South East
where they plan to build more houses
for a million extra noses
pressed to London's
golden window panes

I see this on the telly
whilst I'm waiting for the News
and wonder where they'll put
the drains and hospitals and schools
and how the roads will swallow
all those extra cars.

The telly mutters on again
to show the North's
depopulating
bulldozers gobble up estates
not ten years old

In the plains past Calabozo
we found a snails' graveyard
I'll show you one
next time you come to visit

24. A farewell to the Olympics
❧

The games are over. Life returns again
to normal. Couch potatoes breathe a sigh.
Each day they've watched the fittest and the best
in every sport competing for the gold--
not for its worth in local currency
nor yet because of the residuals--
but for the glory and self-satisfaction which
brings honour to their nation and their name.

The youth of all the world gave of their best,
(two hundred nations represented there).
They ran and jumped and threw, they sailed and
rowed,
they boxed, played tennis, hockey, and football ;
on beams and rings and floor they exercised
gymnastic talents, synchronised they swam;
they lifted weights and wrestled man to man,
they crawled and dived, they rode their horses too.

The camera showed us eyes before the race,
not looking out, but inward, far away,
repeating their own mantras, calm but strong.
The race once won, victorious faces wreathe
themselves in smiles: the unsuccessful pant
and turn away. Some weep. In later years
they'll tell their children's children that
though medal-less they were Olympians.

As viewers turn once more to violence
of cops and robbers nightly on the box
how long will they remember brave athletes
who pulled Achilles tendons in their race
or still competed with a fractured bone,
reluctant to abandon four years' work
and thinking that the glory's worth the pain?
Let's hope they'll soon be fighting fit again!

A couch potato's life is not an easy one
Each morning brings another fight to win
To rise from bed despite the aches and pains
and then to place the body under strain
by standing on one leg to don a sock
and stooping down to tie a double bow.
Time was when changing channels hurt the knees
Remote controls now make the task a breeze.

Hip, hip hooray! For now the games are done--
In four years time, another Marathon

25. Gladiators
❧

A watch-tower dominates the place
Where thousands gather to enjoy the fight;
Two gladiators meeting face to face
With sinews trained especially for the fight.

In Roman times they came with sword or spear
(The Colosseum's where they lost or won)
But nowadays the men with balls appear
To triumph or despair -- at Wimbledon

26. Motorway blues November 2004

This is the story of Barry and John
Schoolmates they were, in times now long gone
They set off one day to visit the school
Barry knows the best way, he's nobody's fool
An hour and a bit should see them safe there
An hour and a half we allowed to be sure
Alas for the boys, Rabby Burns got it right
Plans made by us men oft go up the spout
Past Reigate we sped , not a care in the world
But not too long after our fate was unfurled
Past the turning to Gatwick the traffic got slow
Then ground to a halt, a serious blow
The radio said that a tanker had spilled
All its fuel: the poor driver was killed
An inch at a time we moved now and then
We were glad of the mobile and spoke to the men
Who were hoping to see us at least for the lunch
(In the car we had nothing to drink or to munch)
To hear of this journey may wreathe you in smiles
But it took us SIX HOURS to cover five miles
We missed out the meeting, the lunch and the game
And said to ourselves again and again
We should have been stopped before we were stuck
We blamed it on Them and not on bad luck
Let's hope for the future They learn from that day
And set up a system to keep drivers away
When the motorway's blocked.For example they might
Install at each entry a smart traffic light.
P.S.Our thanks to our wives: their advice on the phone
Made the travellers glad that their wives were at home
Of course they were worried about our surviving
But at least we were saved from their back-seat driving!

27. Thank you, Columbus
❧

He might have pierced the ends
and sucked the goodness out
leaving a perfect shape
but no

He smashed one end
to make it stand
and changed the future
of America

Where once roamed
buffalo, Apache, Kree,
donkeys pump out oil
~ and go to war for it

Today we're more ambitious
warming up
another perfect shape
another future

NOTE. The story was that Columbus,
challenged to stand an egg on its end,
achieved this by bashing it on the table.
True or false, this sets the scene
for today, and global warming

28. David and Goliath

When David slew the giant Philistine
His stone was stronger than Goliath's might.
Millennia have passed -- there's war again
Will stones this time put Israel to flight?

28a. Limerick

There once was a poet from Lim'rick
Who thought he'd discovered the trick
Of writing verses in Erse
But the Erse made them worse
And baffled the people of Lim'rick

29. A Chaucerian Roundel

Tell me about it, if you can
I'd really really like to know
How water changes into snow?

What happened when the world began
A million trillion years ago?
Tell me about it, if you can

Was it part of some Great Plan
That human cleverness should grow
And wipe the earth out with one blow?
Tell me about it, if you can

30. Some thoughts on Identity

1. Literary

I often wonder who I am
Shifting, in the bath, from ham to ham
Quoting that poem by TS Eli--
--ot, looking at my shapely belly

2. Moral

We're all made up of good and bad
My goodness came from Mum and Dad
The badness learnt in later life
Was offset by my loving wife

3. Travel

My ID always used to be my face
Although my body takes more space
Then fingerprints became the thing
As though we're flying to Sing-sing

Now the experts want our eyes
It wouldn't come as a surprise
If later on at borders too
They want a sample of our poo !

31. Poor Jack

His mother smiles at him
as she pushes the pram home.
Jack's face is cold
but he's snug under the blanket
thinking of the milk she's
going to feed him soon.

But now her face is changing
and a shadow man behind her
looks fierce and grunts.
Her sharp scream hurts,
hurts Jack's ears
at each thrust of the knife.

Poor Jack will remember that sound,
that piercing sound,
and the man's face
long after he can no longer
recapture
exactly the way
she used to smile at him

32. A father's boast
❧

Jamie, my son, you make me very proud
to think that you are leader in your field;
In every way you stand out from the crowd
and people tell me that you're quite well-heeled.
You may have learned a thing or two from me,
but found your chances in the world of work;
and now you're top of this important tree
you cook up new ideas and never shirk.
I think you made your breakthrough on the box
by demonstrating all your stuff with flair;
but blow me down, and bless my cotton sox
what cheek ~~ to give advice to Tony Blair !
  And now the food in schools is not half bad
  We Olivers are proud of you, my lad

33. A lament
(for an Andalusian landscape)
❧

How many hundred years the Moors were here
and made us then the gardeners of Spain!
They taught us irrigation, that is clear,
to manage water well, come shine or rain.
Since then five hundred years have passed
And Spain's a nation, part of the E.U.
(a combi-nation meant to last and last
~at least from many people's point of view).
There's talk today of tunnelling the Straits
to link us all to Africa for good.
The global market treats all men as mates
And so we swap technology for food.
    The valley near Facinas, once so fair,
    Is planted now with windmills, farming...air !

34. Conversation piece
❧

Two men in a garden in London town
One called Blair, the other Brown
Sat down as neighbours sometimes may
To settle matters of the day
Said Tony to Gordon I'll be straight
I'm sorry that you've had to wait
but now the time has come for me
to quit the House and leave you free
to learn how different is the game --
numbers and people are not the same.
The folklore says you're a tough nut
That's good if true in general, BUT
Apparently you never listen
Expect your troops to do your bidding
When I was first at number ten
I put around me clever men
Sometimes I told them what to do
Often I listened -- now, will you?
Later on I got the hang
Realised I was top man
And let my fellows talk a bit
Before I told em what was IT
But you are new and so must try
To listen -- think of 'You' not 'I'
Remember if you get it wrong
This could be your last swan song
To you I feel I can confess
That Iraq is a hopeless mess
But as you know, shove comes to push
So long as we depend on Bush
And that is why I'm very pleased

To be his Envoy (Middle East)
For me, that's not a fulltime task
So Gordon please don't hesitate to ask
For guidance from a bloke like me
Or if in doubt just phone Cherie
Here is a special phone in pink
If ever you're in need, just think
The Blairs are at your service there
No extra charge-- as free as air
One secret now I can reveal
You'll never need to talk to Neill
Nor should you believe those silly tales
You read about the prince of Wales
For sensitivity, ask Philip
For wisdom Lilibet's my tip
The public still believe in focus groups:
you know of course they're hocus-pocus

Gordon answered That was nice
I'll bear in mind your wise advice
Now I'll be off to number ten
So pray for me!   Blair said Amen

Home thoughts from abroad
by Robert Browning

O to be in England
now that April's there,
And whoever wakes in England
Sees, some morning, unaware,
That the lowest boughs and the brushwood sheaf
Round the elm-tree bole are in tiny leaf,
While the chaffinch sings on the orchard bough
In England~now!

And after April when May follows,
And the whitethroat builds, and all the swallows!
Hark, where my blossom'd pear-tree in the hedge
Leans to the field and scatters on the clover
Blossoms and dewdrops~at the bent spray's edge~
That's the wise thrush; he sings each song twice over,
Lest you should think he never could recapture
The first fine careless rapture!
And though the fields look rough with hoary dew,
All will be gay when noontide wakes anew
The buttercups, the little children's dower
---Far brighter than this gaudy melon-flower!

Now read on !

35. Home thoughts from abroad ~ today

(with apologies to Robert Browning)

O to be in England,
now that April's there,
And whoever wakes in England
Hears, some morning, unaware
That the traffic's roar drowns the countryside,
Scatt'ring fumes of carbon mon-oxide
While the jet-planes make an extra row
In England~now!

And after April when May arrives,
The traffic's worse, starts taking lives!
Hark, where the wheely-bin right by the hedge
Leans to the road and scatters on the pavement
Rubbish and litter--at the kerbside's edge--
That's the icecream van;it plays each tune twice
over,
Lest you should think he didn't come today
(A week without ice-cream, no way!)
And though the roads look rough with junk and
scum
All will be well when Council lorries come
To sweep it up, and leave the place quite clean
~Until next day, you'd think they'd never been!

Beasts & Dreams

Contents

36. Dream 2000
37. A camel in London
38. Ode on a dead cat's urn
39. If I were a mouse
40. Killer whale
41. Sad day at Llaregyb
42. The wrong road for a humpback whale
43. The day that Rosie got married

36. Dream 2000
❧

Three black triangles below my feet
Cut through the opalescent sea.
The diving raft is moored beyond the tide
Where girls' long legs dangle and swish.
"Don't swim to the raft, John, it's too far'
And I'm 'too young'. When I'm there, the raft
Scratches my tummy as I hoick aboard
And splash the coconut matting. It soon dries
In the perfect sunshine of Before The War.
The raft tilts and sways in the waves
Spins little whirlpools at the corners
And three black triangles below my feet
Cut through the opalescent sea.

Dawn breaks and I remember now
The path pab's test results are due
today.

37. A camel in London

The memorial to the Camel Corps in the Embankment Gardens is a statue of
a camel and rider facing towards the river (near another memorial stone).

A rollicking lolloping camel
Endures the heat of the sun
And he's not averse to a spot of rest
When his long hard day is done

But after a life in the desert
It's a heck of a come-down to be
A bronze in a garden in London
A place where the dogs come to pee

Another thing irks me a little
There's a Camel Corps man on my back
He never says thank-you nor feeds me
Just treats me like any old hack

I don't enjoy living in London
Away from the Sphinx far too far
But on good days at least I can look at
The needle of Cleopatra

38. Ode on a Dead Cat's Urn
❧

(With apologies to John Keats)

Thou dear companion, source of happiness
  Thou purring child of Mrs Cat and Tom
The solemn contours of this urn compress
  Thy feline life more neatly than our rhyme:
What sharp-clawed legend echoed in thy shape
    Of lioness or tiger, or of both,
      In Kashmir or in Africa?
    What kind of men were these whose motor-car
In mad pursuit denied a cat escape?
      What squeal of brakes foretold your destiny?

Ode on a Grecian Urn (part)
❧

by John Keats

Thou still unravished bride of quietness
  Thou foster-child of Silence and slow Time,
Sylvan historian, who canst thus express
  A flowery tale more sweetly than our rhyme:
What leaf-fringed legend haunts about thy shape
    Of deities or mortals, or of both,
      In Tempe or in Arcady?
    What men or gods are these? What maidens loth?
What mad pursuit? What struggle to escape?
    What pipes and timbrels? What wild ecstasy?

39. If I were a mouse

If I were a mouse
I'd live in a house
that was made entirely
of cheese

when I felt like a bite
be it morn, noon or night
I could eat what I jolly
well please

as a matter of habit
I'd cook some welsh rarebit
for breakfast each day of
the week

and on Sunday instead
I'd dry-fry me some ched-
dar with veg to make bubble
and squeak

whenever I choose
stow-away on a cruise
to athens or sydney or
rio

and on Saturday night
I would drink and get tight
and sing songs with gusto and
brie-o

another thing nice
you can say about mice
is the way that they run with
great speed

and mice girls and boys
have no need of toys
'cos they learn very young how
to breed

on a fling to the city
handsome and pretty
they'll stay for a night at the
Hilton

just for a treat
take the best bridal suite
swig champers and nibble on
stilton

but life ain't all roses
bless our paws and pink noses
the facts put me right in
a flap

a hard look at the trends
shows a mouse life soon ends--
natural causes, or worse, in
a trap

it won't happen to me
it won't happen to you
but one day it will happen
to them

40. Killer whale

❧

(with acknowledgments to William McGonagall)

It was the last day of January 2007
A day I will remember until I'm in heaven
Forby in Scotland they were telling the tale
That in the Firth of Forth was seen a killer whale.
Time it was to establish the fact
A man from the BBC sprang into the act
He took a launch and headed North
Up and down the majestic Firth of Forth
Up and down he searched in vain
through storm and wind and gentle rain
But when it was time for him to head for home
To end his day and cease to groan
He saw a great and never-to-be-forgotten sight
Enough to give him a terrible fright
The whale it was he saw it clear
Swimming towards him, getting near
The skipper saw it too, in the nick of time
Which enabled them to survive --
-- and me to compose this rhyme

Beached whale A minke whale stranded itself on a Welsh beach twice in one day...[It was] helped back to sea, but 90 minutes later it was beached again and was put down by a veterinary surgeon.   *The Times 7 March 2007*

41. Sad day at Llaregyb
(with a doff of the cap to Dylan Thomas)

It seems a day like any other
As the sun rises over the sea
silently, blindingly waking the town
To flushings and farts and sweet morning tea.

While sailors ashore may recall Moby Dick
A Minke whale dry-docks on the sand
Sucked in through the wallowing shallows
Helplessly, scratchily, stranded

Councillor Pratt portentously phones
For emergency help ~ 'With immediacy
Send firemen, policemen, lifeboats and cranes
And the Sally Ann van with its buns and hot tea'.

They heave and they puff, they slither and rope
They tug and they heave as the hours groan by
Till the whale floats free in the salt-licking sea
And the men from the Telly heli-copter away

The Fisherman's Arms does a roaring trade
In dark rum (or pale ale) for fireman's throat
But the tide is strong and the Minke is weak
And the tired little whale is dragged back to the beach.

The firemen know and the policemen too
No crane, no lifeboat, ~~ no BBC crew
can save our poor Minke from the arrows of fate
So Councillor Pratt phones his brother, the vet.

Ashes to ashes and deep to deep
This whale's in Wales for death's long sleep

Sunday Times 20 May 07 reports a humpback whale and her calf had swum under the Golden Gate bridge and become land-locked upstream. They both were suffering from propeller cuts, and a whale whisperer was summoned

42. The wrong road for a humpback whale
உ
(with apologies to Robert Frost)

Two ways diverged in a Western sea
And sorry that they could not travel both
And stay on track for where they longed to be
She chose the way under the Bridge, not sea,
But a land-locked passage pointing North

She and her calf had just before
Been injured by a ship -- a shame,
Cut by propeller, oozing gore --
The ship veered suddenly, near the shore
A tragic accident, no cause for blame

Men sent for Bernie Krause that day
The Whisperer famous for his knack
Recording sounds from whales to say
Dear Humpback you have lost your way
Please turn around and hurry back

Her calf'll be telling this tale, ah me!
Somewhere ages and ages hence
Two ways diverged and my mother, she --
She took the one inland from the sea
And that has made all the difference

The road not taken
❧
by Robert Frost

Two roads diverged in a yellow wood
And sorry I could not travel both
And be one traveler, long I stood
And looked down one as far as I could
to where it bent in the undergrowth;

Then took the other, as just as fair,
And having perhaps the better claim,
Because it was grassy and wanted wear;
Though as for that, the passing there
worn them really about the same,

And both that morning equally lay
In leaves no step had trodden black.
Oh, I kept the first for another day!
Yet knowing how way leads on to way,
I doubted if I should ever come back.

I shall be telling this with a sigh
Somewhere ages and ages hence:
Two roads diverged in a wood, and I --
I took the one less traveled by,
And that has made all the difference

43. The day that Rosie got married
𝖈𝖆𝖛

The day that Rosie got married
She had the most terrible dream
She woke with a sweat and a shudder
And emitted a ladylike scream

In her dream she was walking a tightrope
High above the Niagara Falls
She was watched by a crowd of old women
Who were all wearing black knitted shawls

Now when you are crossing Niagara
It's tricky enough on your own
But young Rosie was followed by Mother
Which caused her to say with a groan:

'Dear Mother, you know it's MY wedding
You know that Jack Husband is mine
If only you'd leave us together
I'm sure it'll all work out fine.'

They say that good company's two
While three is a crowd or some-such
But when you are walking a tight-rope
Even one more than one is too much!

Now Rosie was using a pole
To help her to balance, you see,
So that turning to talk to her mother
She caught her a blow on the knee

Her mother turned pale at this blow
And clutched at her knee with a cry
"But Rosie, you sholuldn't have hit me
Es-pecially when we're so high.'

The tight-rope was starting to wobble
A dangerous moment for all
If the wobble got very much worse
They'd be in for sickening fall!

'Stand still, Mother dear' she admonished
'Stop clutching your knee, and don't cry
If this rope continues to wobble
We'll be falling right out of the sky

Then the wedding would have to be cancelled
And instead of marrying Jack
I would be stuck on the shelf
AND THE PRESENTS WOULD
HAVE TO GO BACK !

This steadied the nerve of dear Mother
Who had prayed for this day all her life
When she could be queen of the party
Whilst making her daughter a wife

The crowd had grown silent in wonder
As the two women swayed overhead
They knew it was really quite dang'rous
With one little slip they'd be dead

When almost across Rosie started
To dance a small Charleston for joy
For she knew she would go all the way
And be married to her fav'rite boy

Distracted by this sudden movement
Rosie's mother looked down at her feet
Saw the fierce rushing waters below them
And her face turned as white as a sheet

Mother called out to Rosie for succour
And Rosie turned quickly to see
And round came her pole just as quickly
Gave a heck of a clout on Mum's knee

Poor Mother she wasn't a gymnast
And couldn't help giving a lurch
Lost her balance completely for ever
And fell, in a word, from her perch.

The crowd held their breath at her tumble
Then screamed when they saw she was dead
And Rosie screamed too when she noticed
That the waters below had turned red.

That scream woke up Rosie at last
And she leapt from her bed with a cheer
For today WAS the day of her wedding
To Jack Husband, her very own dear

Whimsy

Contents

44. Omphalos
45. Twang
46. Feet
47. Hands
48. I never thought I'd be a Gran
49. The pram is in the river
50. Embankment Garden Statue
51. A visit to the cleaners
52. October
53. The magic jar

44. Omphalos

iddell & Scott's Greek lexicon states--*Omphalos, the navel, Latin umbilicus. Anything 'e a navel:-Delphi was called omphalos as the navel or centre of the earth.* ome early Christian painters showed Adam and Eve, logically, without navels.

An ode to the belly-button

I'm not like Shakespeare's lover--
Sighing (with an ode to his mistress' eyebrow).
Joyful praise I sing -- to that human scar,
the midwife's love-knot, lifelong reminder
of every body's Day of Birth,
the navel.
Omphalos in ancient Greece,
Delphi, centre of the earth.
You are an oasis
on the belly's globe,
You are a deep secret
of the obese,
a flaunted feature
of the nubile young,
a well to gather
sweat from honest toil.
You are contemplative,
fluff-collector,
universal feature of
the human race,
mimick'd by the pregnant orange.

Poor Eve! Poor Adam, too!
Was it for want of navels
That they took the apple?

Thoughts on a word used by Surtees
in his account of the visit Jorrocks made
to Newmarket -- or, put more simply:

45. Twang

In eighteen-thirty Surtees wrote
The coachman *twanged* his horn
He didn't *sound* his warning note
Nor *blow* the passengers to warn

The point that I am making now
Words change the changing times to suit
We do not *twang* or *sound* or *blow*
Our horns today -- we *toot*

But twang's a verb we should revive
Maybe a form of singing
Or then a brand new way to jive
To get the youngsters swinging

Would you like to twang with me
I asked the lady fair
I cannot understand why she
Stayed fixed upon her chair

Yes, Surtees wrote in olden time
About a jaunt for Jorrocks
Can anyone suggest a rhyme
That I could use for Jorrocks?

46. Feet

Feet are used in many ways
I will therefore sing their praise
If this concept makes you bleat
Now's the time -- vote with your feet

When naughty children misbehave
You put your foot down if you're brave
But if you're driving fast from town
You'll likely put your foot right down

If speed-dating is your show
Footloose and fancy-free you go
But be careful~~ in a minute
You may put your foot right in it.

When you enter in a race
Best foot forward you should place
Paradoxically though
Feet first is a clumsy way to go

Humans think two feet are great
Ants have six and spiders eight
Will you please think long and hard
What has three feet? Yes, a yard.

Another thing I've always found
I like my my feet upon the ground
But one thing's sure, succeed or blunder
We'll all end up, some six feet under

47. Hands
ॐ

Hands are used for many a thing
Their praises therefore I will sing.
They're versatile, it seems to me;
Pray, raise your hands, if you agree.
But if in battle (or in sport)
you are not winning as you ought,
--in fact you're losing--, with a frown
you may admit you've lost hands down

Speaking of down, how great's the cost
if shipping with all hands is lost;
while if economy you crave,
wear hand-me-downs -- you're sure to save
A hand has many different points
Thumbs and fingers, knuckle joints
'All fingers and thumbs' they say I am
Yet never call me handy man

In gangster films is it true
they stick em up with superglue?
Boys on bikes quite often shout
'Look, no hands' and then 'Look out!'
The poor may live from hand to mouth
Bridge hands are dealt to North and South
But if the squire a-kissing tries,
'Un-hand me, Sir!' the damsel cries

Duerer it was who showed great flair
In drawing human hands at prayer,
but best of all for me, my dove,
is holding hands to show our love

48. I never thought I'd be a Gran
&

I never thought I'd be a Gran

Was born a boy, grew up a man

Married a wife -- by procreation

We added to the population

(The years went by, gosh how they sped!

Our boy grew up and then got wed

Last week his wife produced a daughter.)

My life change came from drinking water

It seems that water from the mains

Is now recycled from the drains

And this includes bits from the Pill

which take effect -- make Jack a Jill.

Where once was tough testosterone

Is now a feminine hormone

And that is why, no more a man,

I've changed my sex to be a Gran

49. The pram is in the river
❧

The pram is in the river
I wonder why it's there
I hope it's 'cos the kids have grown--
It's not needed any more

But just suppose a baby's died
And baby stuff's not wanted
Then nearly-daddy might have cleared
The nursery and dumped it

More likely though it's kids again
Who used the pram for transport
Until the game seemed dull one day
And they launched this floating target

The saddest thought of all is this
The owner was a bag lady
Her food, her bed, her all was there
Until she joined her Maker

The pram is in the river
I know exactly why:
Its spokes are bust, it doesn't go,
Heigh ho, it had to die!

50. Embankment Garden Statue

❧

Arthur Sullivan

e's just a bronze bust, on a granite plinth, facing away from the river,
vards the Savoy, scene of his triumphs. Standing half-draped and weeping
ainst the plinth is a Muse, Edwardian profile and bosom bared in grief.)

Euterpe, why do you shed tears for me?
My music will live on for all to hear
Until the sun sets on the Empire, or
Mikado's motors make the English cheer!

Come dry your eyes, turn up your face to mine
And let me see your eyes. This poor bronze bust
Which stand in classic form on granite plinth
Can never love again, nor even lust.

'Tis I should weep, frustrated as I gaze
Sadly Savoy-wards, cursing all day long
The bitter rows I had with Gilbert there
He led with words; I followed with my song.

Enough of that! My gloom is overdone
Let's drink a toast in champers or in beer!
Euterpe, pray you, shed no tears for me
My music will live on for all to hear

51. A visit to the cleaners

Going to the shops is nothing new
The bank, the chemists's shop and Somerfield,
But then I had another thing to do
Collect a blouse I'd left to have it cleaned.
That's when I saw her working at the back
Her iron skims across the work so fast
It's obvious she's really got the knack,
Until it's time for her to pause at last --
The iron's at rest, she stretches, makes no sound
Just shakes her hair as though she's been in rain
Then rubs her nose and rubs it round and round
Once more as if to screw it on again
   That moment stays with me: I guess it shows
   The job's okay, but plays the devil with her nose

52. October

Our tenth month calls itself October
This seems to me a terrible mis-nomer
For 'oct' words normally mean eight
And calendars are meant to tell it straight

It would be weird, I think you will agree
If, one day, swimming in the sea
You meet an octopus and then
Discover that his feet add up to ten*

Or then again, if music is your bag
Wrong numbers can create a fearful snag
Enough to make a keen composer fret --
I have to write ten parts for this Octet?!

But putting these semantics on one side
My feelings for October I can't hide
It is the month when I first saw the light
No wonder that it gives me such delight

Now is the time to turn the heating on
Autumn is here and summer's really gone
The leaves are turning yellow, gold and red
And most will fall before the month is dead

When candles lit inside our pumpkins glow
They say that witches may be on the go;
They fly on broomsticks, have no need of feet
But ring the doorbell begging 'Trick or treat"

*PS I have since read in Jonathan Raban's book, Passage to Juneau, that "...in the depths of Puget Sound...the Pacific giant squid *Moroteuthis robusta* has ten hooked ntacles." Come to think of it, they aren't called octacles !

53. The magic jar

I'll tell you the tale of a magic jar
It'll interest you, whoever you are
'cos the magic in the jar was such
that I could tell, however much
the people tried to hide,
just what went on inside their mind.
I found the jar upon a tip
and took it home to polish it
and when I took the stopper out
the pong from it went up my snout.
By chance I had the wireless on
at newstime when the interviewer John
 asking politicians for their views
(as if their words are always news)
and suddenly John's questions stung
like horseflies rising from the dung
The answers were a different kind
like cream and oil to soothe your mind.
At half past eight it looked like rain
as I went off to catch the train.
The tube was crowded as it is,
back to back and phiz to phiz,
and so I stood and looked at faces
mostly lacking airs or graces.
Amongst the crowd is a young pair
their thoughts are wafting on the air
the girl is dreaming, makes no sound,
sees pink rose petals all around
while he thinks as a young man may
of romping naked in the hay.

Next to them a businessman
with briefcase and a striking tan
is scheming how to get the gold
before his time is up -- too old!
Further on in this same carriage
I see a priest who dreams of marriage
to a girl all dressed in red
with wicked horns upon her head
but then the priest turns up his eyes
to where his guardian angel flies.
And next I watch a soldier's back
his mind is sweating in Iraq
and, looking at a bearded man,
suspects he's from Afghanistan.
An office girl smartly dressed
doesn't like that she is pressed
beside a workman wearing jeans
ruddy-faced and full of beans.
Beside him is a beardless youth
of doubtful gender -- it's the truth --
who finds it difficult to choose
between the cleavage of her bloose
or, just like in a Whitehall farce,
the cleavage of the workman's arse!
All this I saw and much much more
the day I found and sniffed that jar.
And there's a moral to this tale
Carve it on stone, write it in Braille,
Think what you may, it ain't ideal
to tell the world just what you feel

Romance

Contents

54. Absence
55. A touch of class
56. La Ronde
57. My wife
58. A thank-you note
59. Crying
60. First love
61. Anniversary
62. The month of May
63. A Christmas proposal
64. My darling wife

54. Absence

Dear love, I wish that I could see your face.
Now we've been parted for an hour or two
it seems an eon since you left this place
and I am aching for a sight of you.
My memory's so weak it is unfair
I cannot hold your beauty in my mind
Your face,your smiling eyes, your mouth, your hair
all melt and disappear as though I'm blind
This photo ought to keep my love alive
it shows your features clearly as it should
That afternoon I took you for a drive
And we made love sweet naked in the wood
     But pictures hurt by showing what I miss
     When you're not here for me to hold and kiss

55. A touch of class

You lovely girl, I wish I was a poet
'cos when I saw you in the pub that night
I think I fell in love, in fact I know it
I promise you I wasn't even tight.
You came with half a dozen other guys
who swamped the bar and made a lot of noise
Right on I loved the sparkle in your eyes
and that you drank a pint just like the boys.
Your jeans clung on your fanciable arse
your bellybutton winked a shining gem
in ev'ry way you showed a touch of class
and then you left the pub again -- with them.
    Just ships we were, yeah, passing in the night:
    you came, you went, you conquered me all right

56. La ronde
❧

Edwardian young ladies put their hair up
Before they could let it down.
With the War came the Flappers who giggled away
And eyed all the soldiers in town.

The Twenties brought 'IT' girls
Some of whom were quite fast;
Sex Appeal in the Thirties
Was mentioned at last

In wartime again the Yanks were fresh over here
And aggressively over-sexed
But peace reunited the married once more
And millions of babies came next

The Sixties were swinging
With minis galore
As the Pill came along
To open the door...

...for AIDS to appear
As a signal to all
That there may be a price
for having a ball

57. My wife
☙

(Provoked by 'Free Union' by Andre Breton)

My wife whose laughter is a blackbird's song
Whose smile is sunshine on an icy day
Whose lips are soft as thistledown
Whose chin bears resolution's thrust
Whose being is a world above the stars for me
My wife whose love's a compass in the fog
Whose focus lights on others not on her
Whose fingers could remake a spider's web
Whose mind's a jewel set in golden commonsense
Whose spirit effervesces over all

58. A thank you note
☙

(for a jug designed as a female nude)

Dear Daughter,

       I sit at my desk
       can't think what to write
       my mind is a blank
       but there in my sight
       are two jugs on a jug
       of a beautiful blue
       and I recall the fun
       we had making you

          love and thanks,

            Papa

59. Crying

ॐ

July 1996

What makes a grown man feel enough to cry?

Is it the death of millions in Ruanda's war,
Or children mutilated by their dad
For richer begging on some Bombay street?

Is it the wasting death of gentle men
Permitted to be gay, to die of AIDS,
Or trapped by drugs to dirty needle's end?

The victim of a rape? who hears it said
'She asked for it. She's old enough to know
That after midnight he'd expect her to...'

The grisly diggings of some Bosnian field
That will for ever reek of dragon's teeth
Does that evoke a tear, or even two?

I'm sure it should, buit somehow it does not.

But when I saw a fifteen-year-old girl
Come back to win the doubles tournament
It's silly, but today that made me cry.

60. First Love

In all the centuries since Time began
No one had ever felt like this before,
As we lay wrapped together on your bed
    Lip to lip, skin on skin,in the lap of heaven

When first we met, your smile lasso'd my gaze,
The sparkle in your eyes, your generous mouth,
And what a tingle rushed straight to my heart
    The day you slipped your hand so easily in mine !

Do you remember when we planned to meet
Outside the cinema straight after work
And how you didn't come for two whole hours
    Because some crisis kept you foully late

The agony of waiting for you there
My looking, pacing, phoning -- no reply,
Was washed away the moment you arrived
    To show that you were safe and cared for me.

When that last night we knew, no matter what,
Your ship would take you far away from me,
Did you feel too that heaven was leaving us,
    Extinguishing the fires we'd stoked so hot?

When interfering dawn pushed in the room,
I butterfly'd your eyelashes with mine
Made tears to drop and fill the corner buds
    Where your sweet eyelids met -- do you recall?

The arrangement was you'd telephone at noon
The day your ship was due to leave these shores:
One last good-bye before you crossed the world,
    And separated us through Space and Time

That day was longer than ten lifetimes, whole
Eternity. My desk a battlefield
Littered with wounded thoughts, dead hopes,
    And piercing memories -- your touch, your taste.

Do you remember that you never rang?

61. Anniversary

John took the empty beer-can
and crushed it in his fist
Popped open yet another
looked towards the TV screen
Brooding on what might have been

Mary set the dining table
with silver glass and china
Sweet Williams in the centre
and a red candle lit

She poured the wine
Tossed back her hair
and with a wry smile
raised her glass
To my *darling* John--
Thank God he's gone!

62. The month of May

This month, the month of May, was merry once
So Shakespeare says and he's no dunce
He wrote It was a lover and his lass
With a hey nonny no (or a hey nonny YES?)
The young folk danced around the village green
Their maypole decked in ribbons bright and clean
The girls had flowers woven in their hair
The squire provided cakes and ale to spare
Then later under many a greenwood tree
She loved to lie with he, and he with she
It was the time when Cupid held full sway
It was the very merry month of May
    Are things the same, the same for us today?
    Of course I think they are, Hip Hip Hooray!

63. A Christmas Proposal

Shall I compose a Christmas rhyme for thee?
To tell of all the presents I would bring
To lay beneath your gaily baubled tree --
Rich cakes, and wine, and best of all this Ring.
How else can I to thee the message tell
That I love thee and I long thee to wed
To make days merry as a wedding bell
And nights the heav'n where we would share our bed?
This golden Ring's a symbol of the time
That we should spend together: all our life,
Bodies and souls in harmony sublime,
I as your husband, you my loving wife
    If we were wed ,thou would'st for nothing lack
    I pray that thou dost not this Ring send back

64. My darling wife
❧

I could not love you more, my darling heart
If I were twice the man and you a queen
I could not bear for us to live apart
For fear we'd think our love had never been
But now we are together all the time
From dusk to dawn and all day long as well
Some moments fall far short of the sublime
Why this has come to pass I cannot tell
Is it because the senses dull with age,
Familiarity may breed contempt?
(I'll put the question to a famous sage)
Or was the love God gave us only lent?
    One thing is certain in my long, long life
    You are the best of all, my darling wife

INDEX--poems are numbered, pages are not!

Growing up
1. This little girl
2. Life's journey
3. Christmas Eve
4. Summer 1938
5. Prep school
6. Thankyou Sir
7. An ordinary boy
8. Resolutions
9. A troubador I'd like to be

Life & death
10. A nun's tale
11. Flanders July 2005
12. Onions
13. Blessing
14. Mummy wasn't ill...
15. The clouds are grand
16. Thanks
17. Duck thieves
18. Landfall
19. Holiday video
20. No choice at Dunblane

O tempora
21. Thought for today
22. Immigrants
23. Evolution
24. A farewell to the Olympics
25. Gladiators
26. Motorway blues
27. Thankyou Columbus
28. David & Goliath
29. Chaucerian Roundel
30. Some thoughts on Identity
31. Poor Jack
32. A father's boast
33. A lament
34. Conversation piece
35. Home thoughts from abroad

Beasts & Dreams
36. Dream 2000
37. A camel in London
38. Ode on a dead cat's urn
39. If I were a mouse
40. Killer whale
41. Sad day at Llaregyb
42. The wrong road for a humpback whale
43. The day Rosie got married

Whimsy
44. Omphalos
45. Twang
46. Feet
47. Hands
48. I never thought I'd be a Gran
49. The pram is in the river
50. Embankment Garden Statue
51. A visit to the cleaners
52. October
53. The magic jar

Romance
54. Absence
55. A touch of class
56. La Ronde
57. My wife
58. A thank-you note
59. Crying
60. First love
61. Anniversary
62. The month of May
63. A Christmas proposal
64. My darling wife